W9-CII-780

STRAND PRICE
5 00
4 23

YUNHEE MIN

MILES
McENERY
GALLERY

511 West 22nd Street
New York NY 10011

515 West 22nd Street
New York NY 10011

525 West 22nd Street
New York NY 10011

520 West 21st Street
New York NY 10011

ISLAND OF THE SENSES

By Nick Herman

After all, love takes place in the world.

—Alain Badiou[1]

Entering the studio of Yunhee Min is an experience I liken to wading. One wades into the medium and process of her making, surrounded on all sides by paintings and tests on paper; works in progress; containers of paint of every description, in varying viscosities; and what might be understood as ongoing experiments. Experiments in the spirit of an old laboratory, where material undergoing transformation takes time to develop, and the old motto of the alchemist holds sway: *solve et coagula*, dissolve and distill.[2]

Min's vibrant surfaces and inchoate materials surround you; they're on the walls, of course, large powerful works on canvas with complex combinations of shape and color that command space, but also on the floor and tables throughout. Indeed, the process favored by the artist to build up her compositions is one that utilizes very liquid paint (paint that must be applied horizontally so it stays in place until dry). So, one wades into multiple planes of process, the studio becoming a kind of terrain into which the artist enters.

To wade comes from the Old English word *wadan*, "to move onward" and also "penetrate," from a Germanic word meaning "go (through)." The word, obviously, is used most often to suggest water, and to my ear, immersion; one wades into the deep. A transitive verb, it conveys viscosity, time, and the way one's own watery body is a hybrid medium that refuses to abide by stable borders. It is in this spirit of hybridity, both ontological and corporeal, that I wish to write about Min's new work, for to engage with the artist is to immediately be in a dialogue on multiple material levels and also to find oneself enmeshed in a deeply philosophical framework.

WET

Yunhee Min is perhaps best known for her use of distinctive tools to lay down broad swaths of paint in abstract and vivid fields, and she has been negotiating the resultant configurations and juxtapositions for more than two decades—building up an expansive body of work that balances her primary medium of painting with a companion interest in architecture and site-specificity. Within this approach to making work and corralling color, she has often spoken of the interface between the tool and her body, returning again and again to the limitations of her reach, the arc of her arm to define gesture; respiration, and its impact on creative toil; and, of course, site as metonymic. This interest in limits, in turn, has set into motion an expansive and regenerative process of experimentation where the act of painting is a performance and stress test, a calculated balancing of energy, media, ground, apparatus, space, scale, mood, and, ultimately, chance.

The act of recording the body in this way, of using paint to lay down haptic tracks and mix time as embodied by coagulated pigment, can be understood as philosophical in scope, mapping how objects and actions relate to one another. But it is also related to sound, an abiding inspiration for the artist. Sound in this way can be understood as a register of energy, a manifestly *fluid state* that constitutes what the philosopher Gilles Deleuze calls the "machine of desire" that, when aroused, results in what he designates as "territory" or site being established—as in a painting.[3] It is this protean conversation, about the tension between territory (depicted as line, border, edge, mark, field) and wetness, as both solvent and catalyst, that Min takes up.

Untraditional tools that have become synonymous with Min's painting practice speak to this kind of prosthetic logic and playful *entendre*; chief among them are the roller, squeegee, rag, and spray bottle. But she also uses tubs of all sizes to mix colors, not just to the desired hue, but consistency, and diverse surfaces to allow for the horizontal application of paint so that the watery media can slowly dehydrate, as well as spread out and run. Indeed, this issue of paint flow and containment is paramount, as the thin paint Min uses would, if applied vertically, immediately drip, thereby evoking gravity as the chief vector. Instead, for Min, the primary element is time, and within the infinite densities of her watery medium there lies the secret to how she is able to create such dynamic compositions, exploiting the way drying and opacity harmonize *to make time visible*. By refusing any telltale painterly marks, and by actively cultivating saturation and entropy as gesture, Min is able to unwind her creative process. In short, she reanimates the paint, in a sense rewilding her compositions and infusing them with latency. In this respect, she adopts Joan Didion's memorable turn of a phrase "play it as it lays,"[4] infusing the works with an erotic charge and agency that underlies Elizabeth Grosz's assertion that "art is the sexualization of survival."[5]

Steeped in chromatic hues and muted tones, Min's work suggests this ripe fusion between ontology and biology. There is a whiff of both contagion and coquetry, as her colors bleed and bloom (not for nothing do we call bold colors "loud"), and for the artist this allusion can be linked in part to her study of Roger Caillois, whose writing on mimesis challenges the rigid borders between science, philosophy, and art. For Caillois, play in particular can be understood as marrying objective experimentation with the less tangible poetic and performative impulses that divine and evince attraction in nature. Made up of four parts, Agon (conflict), Mimicry, Alea (chance) and Ilinx (whirlpool/vertigo), Caillois' framework speaks directly to how Min's paintings merge the beguiling mixing of color with physical process to become a kind of territorializing event reminiscent of animal display.[6] Min asserts this power to mark, not through any compulsion but through something decidedly more cool, a kind of ritual engineering, setting up an experiment and then stepping back to see its outcome. Evoking the original measure known as the fathom, Min uses the properties of water to establish and conceptualize space relative to her own body in a consort that is less *seductive* than *inductive*.[7] As such, her colors attract and repel like magnetic forces, compelling the viewer to navigate a painting's complex trajectories and spatial configurations—again with an emphasis on territory as synonymous with life force.

The physical traces left by a desiring body imbues the current works on display at Miles McEnery Gallery, where the artist has focused again on the roller as a surrogate probe. Using the roller allows Min to do two things: lay down parallel and overlapping planes of color, and also use the mechanism itself to leave an echo of its use—the repetitive footprint of its spinning, nappy roll. The device allows Min to build up a secondary record of discernible rhythm. The roller move can be read in nearly all the works in the gallery, evoking not just the stuttering hand of the artist but familiar if arcane devices for projection and reproduction. Indeed, there is a canny resemblance of the vertical traces of the roller face to ubiquitous

media artifacts, such as the sprocket holes on 35mm film or a malfunctioning printer. In these and other proprioception analogies there is again the assertion of time as mostly a measure of mediation, and the logic of design as implicit in even the simplest animal motion.

It is this combination of the tool and its technological *signature* that links Min's practice not just to a history of painting and sound but to what Deleuze explores as *difference*: i.e., forces that emerge and animate life.[8] Manifesting physically, on what he calls a plane of immanence, this assertion of material difference can be best understand as vibration, a technical term that links music and color where repetition becomes legible in what he labels a *refrain*, "a prism, a crystal of space-time. [The refrain] acts upon that which surrounds it, sound or light, extracting from it various vibrations, or decompositions, projections, or transformations."[9] Registering this difference, recording both its loudest and most subtle permutations, is the job of a tuned instrument, and in this way recording the difference might also be said to be a game of listening, a comparison that for Min has roots in her fond memories of playing Go as a child with her father. For the artist, the game's pieces (called stones) offered a first introduction to how color can be used to designate space and delimit time, as the play would often carry on over days without any clear winner taking shape. A game that evokes strategy but also something more innate, even instinctual, Go introduced Min to patiently waiting for the picture to find its own equilibrium, which anticipated her studio process of letting the painting evolve and prefigured her interest in philosophy.

To really see Min's project at work is to see this instrumental role of her composition as a kind of resonator or *pickup*, as it is within this analogy of amplification that sound can be understood as synonymous with painting. And there is an important if sometimes oversimplified relationship between the artist and the scientist that rests in part on the way both roles require training to hone a principle— to distinguish characteristics or timbre. This process is one that is key for Min, although not because she advocates for virtuosity or pure data, but quite the contrary, because of her abiding interest in creating space for the amplification to occur.

One strategy Min uses to frame this idea of amplification is to repeat patterns in her work. A mark, like that of the roller, may be picked up and inserted in another part of the painting, or responded to, such as when she blocks in the negative space formed between her rolled tracks. In this way, Min is engaging not only with a formal process, but with one that can be likened to a spatialized call and response, very much like that in Go. Standing before Min's paintings one is immersed in this kind of nuanced game of cat and mouse.

In a body of work, such as in *New Paintings*, one sees what appear to be rhyming elements in different paintings. Whether through color pairings or experimental residue there is a kind of relationality, one sees patterns and colonizing outposts, and effervescent intersections and cloned attributes coalesce in pools of sister shapes. This can be seen clearly for example in the radiant fluorescent green forms that mark the right side of *Round and Round* (2022) and the similar if more shadowy versions of the same forms visible on the left side. A person could project any number of symbolic interpretations here—totem, insect burrow, architectural fortification— but what is most palpable is their sharing of some DNA. They are related and evolving within the scope of the painting and beyond; there is an equally unconstrained track of muddy yellow creeping along the edge of *Blue Moon* (2022) and an even more virulent deep blue proliferation in *Wild is the Wind* (2022). Are these shapes not in effect occupying their environs and asserting agency by establishing territory?

In this way, Min seems to play with the potential that her paintings could constitute an ecology or, to strain the metaphor, an orchestration—both a single picture and part of a complex cycle. Seeing the suspended particulate matter in this way, there is a direct if fuzzy correlation to a scientific method, a sequencing of material traits—what Caillois sees in the frozen facets of stones and lying hidden in the whirlpool of *Ilinx*. And here again, it must be said there is an ontological suggestion, however obscure, linking evolution and consciousness to watery depths and permeability.

DRY

According to Bruno Latour, the advent of science in the West is rooted in the Enlightenment ideal of purification, a proposition that differentiates between rational thought, as embodied by empiricism and objective instrumentation, and nature, as symbolized by superstition. This, he contends in his book *We Have Never Been Modern* (1991), is a false and unsustainable bifurcation that is simply not an honest rendering of material reality. Instead, Latour suggests, we should reevaluate our modern technologies, including art, acknowledging the presence of earlier, more primitive belief systems.

This focus on the apparatus of science and the way tools influence and embed themselves into our systems of belief is a powerful if elided aspect in Min's work that further establishes the political underpinnings of her aesthetic. Indeed, her interest in unorthodox colors, in reusing "old/outdated" or muddy pigments, in mixing and copying tones intuitively, and in recycling marks across different paintings and over entire bodies of work subtly confronts the central premise of painting as modern.[10] In this way, Min embraces the subjective intimacy and relative psychological complexity often associated with mythology or even mysticism,[11] while still insisting on the relative vacuity of the mood that her synthetic colors contain or are marketed to fulfill.[12] In doing so, she destabilizes both the saccharine interpretation of abstraction and its opposite pole, rationalism. As the artist herself points out, she is much more comfortable with the notion of Kantian beauty than she is with its antithesis, the sublime. And, as I have alluded to before, this refusal to allow the painting to be merely pretty or heroic can in some large measure be linked to Min's almost intuitive reliance on pollution as a device. By insisting that we see the instability of material in its wet/dry cycle, the artist seems to evoke a profound observation about evolution and history, mirroring Latour, that art contains its predecessors in vestigial and vernacular echoes. For Min, the watery, worked-over marks and chemical tracks hover over this metaphor of extraction and colonization, not critiquing distinct cultural signifiers but as germs (a different kind of culture) that infect, proliferate, and ultimately destabilize.

The analogy of recycling—an organic process more akin to composting than appropriation—is crucial here, tying back to the Deleuzian concept of difference/repetition. When combined with the refrain of the tool itself, this secondary resonance of paint as somehow a systemic by-product of industry, a discharge or tailing, connects Min to the pioneering science of Donna Haraway, whose writing she often evokes in conversation. For Haraway, the social and ecosystemic crises we face, which are contextualized by Latour's analysis of Western history, require human consciousness to confront what she calls "trouble," a concept that informs the title of her eponymous book *Staying with the Trouble* (2016), where art and science require an acknowledgment that our "pastpresentfuture processes and entities of the earth— not the earth as mother, but the earth as our flesh and we its flesh…is always tentacularly entangled in composing and decomposing worlds."[13] This very liquid knotted relationality is for Haraway a kind of intelligence where, in the words of the artist Jeff Wall, "…the liquids study us, even from a great distance."[14]

For Min, the slippery analogy of embodiment as premised on permeability and impurity links her aesthetic to this deeper, less orthodox scientific analysis. Indeed, her use of vertical bands to create compositional time is reminiscent of maps and strata, but there is something more off-kilter; perhaps echoing Wall, the paintings are alive, their staccato trails snaking across the canvas, their edges blending and disappearing into one another to suggest subterranean, even alien, worlds. This latter allusion, a comparison that lies at the surface of Min's recursive lines, seems to suggest a kind of din, a cacophonous thrum of harmony and dissonance in ways evoking insect chatter or echolocation. Indeed, Min seems to highlight how notation as the basis for transcribing sound can be understood as an often-overlooked companion to abstraction. To extend Latour's thesis, the art of surviving (and surveying) the wild is a knowledge base still very much in evidence in Min's work. This complex overlapping of symbol and system can be seen clearly in *Play it as it Lays* (2022) the largest work in the show, where the snake pattern suggests this refrain of cyclical regeneration and skin as listening device.

In paintings that are often in conversation with one another and seem to suggest an extended ecological interpretation, this sense of being connected, a flow of call and response, links Haraway to the philosopher Elizabeth Grosz, who writes in her chapter "Animals, Sex, and Art:"

> "While the conditions and raw materials for art are located within territory, as part of the earth, they become art, architecture, dance only to the extent they become transportable elsewhere; that they intensify bodies that circulate, move, change; in that they too become subject to evolutionary transformation and spatial and temporal movement."[15]

By animating the material of art itself and, by extension, embracing the more radical underpinnings of the scientific method, Grosz points again to a fundamental force in Min's paintings: that the paint remains alive (equally marked by the many environmental variables it is subjected to, as it is the original raw materials and life cycles that constitute its distilled body) and that a painting's particles and pigmented coagulations travel through space a vibrational refrain within viewers as they view the work. This is a measure of the artist and her world. Another recording. Another fathom.

As such, Min's paintings can suggest the site that closely echoes the body across almost all environmental conditions and species, that of a nest or den. As animals, we cluster and draw materials around us, and the den reflects our reach. And these gestures of framing and announcing our bodies are repeated nightly, seasonally, and across time, linking different species and amplifying their relationships via the gathered media that marks their physical territory. In this way, architecture reflects a cyclical process that (re)infuses nonliving stuff with life, animating the inanimate and, in Haraway's words, "composing and decomposing worlds."

This argument for an evolution, and more pointedly *an ethic*, based on one's physical relationship to a specific environment or media and for the symbiosis that remains at its heart,[16] is the basis for Grosz's reading of the seminal ethologist Jakob von Uexküll, who argues, "The problem of life is the problem of design…life is artistic in the biological forms it induces, in the variations, in pattern of living it generates." A hyper-spatialized call and response, Uexküll evokes this principle as based on "musical laws of nature," highlighting how creativity reflects a spatial awareness, what he calls an organism's *umwelt* or "island of the senses." Min's paintings, alive and awash in color, evoke both her own radical pleasure and the unconstrained excess that imbues wild life. They mime Uexküll's famous idea that, "the body of an animal is an inverted map of its world."[17]

For Uexküll and Grosz, as with Latour and Haraway, there is a dialogue that is unfolding and in time, in which "each living creature is a series of 'tonal' responses to various 'melodies' played by its *umwelt*, through various performances it undertakes….These tones make particular objects in its wild drinkable, editable, walkable, sittable and so on…."[18] In Min's *New Paintings*, recording this animating principle produces a liberating effect, inspiring not only a vocabulary of relationality but of mystery and the unexpected, where all living things are "tuned" to their environments. It is this humming attunement that governs the paintings on display, each of which can be understood as containing this insistent liquid desire. ∎

Nick Herman is an artist and writer living in Los Angeles, CA.

Endnotes

1. Alain Badiou with Nicolas Truong, *In Praise of Love* (New York: The New Press, 2009), p. 35.

2. For a well-researched and inspired reading of alchemy see Peter Lamborn Wilson, Christopher Bamford, and Kevin Townley, *Green Hermeticism: Alchemy and Ecology* (Great Barrington, MA: Lindisfarne Books, 2007.

3. Min often cites Giles Deleuze as an early influence, and in this essay I have used the writings of Elizabeth Grosz to read into Deleuze in a way that I feel opens the conversation and connects powerfully to Min's work.

4. In the course of our conversations Min decided to adopt this phrase as one of her titles in the show.

5. Elizabeth Grosz, *Chaos, Territory, Art: Deleuze and the Framing of the Earth* (New York: Columbia University Press, 2008).

6. Marina Warner, "The Writing of Stones: Roger Caillois' Imaginary Logic," *Cabinet 29* (Spring 2008). https://www.cabinetmagazine.org/issues/29/

7. A fathom was originally a measure of a person's outstretched arms. It speaks to control and capital, suggesting navigable waters, thereby establishing a link between colonization and bodily projection as exploit.

8. Elizabeth Grosz, *Becoming Undone: Darwinian Reflections on Life, Politics, and Art* (Durham, NC: Duke University Press, 2011), pp. 26-27.

9. Elizabeth Grosz, *Chaos, Territory, Art: Deleuze and the Framing of the Earth* (New York: Columbia University Press, 2008), p. 57.

10. For more on how Min's work relates to the history of commercial color, see Jan Tumlir's essay "Yunhee Min: The Pass, the Band, the Color" (2014). Yunheemin.com/media/gallery/files/ESSAY_JT.pdf

11. This might not be the correct word, as Min has never alluded to any specific interest in mysticism. However, as opposed to totemism, or even the more chaste symbolism, mysticism seems to at least honestly acknowledge the way color shares roots with both medicine and, well, mysticism; furthermore, it nods toward water as a medium of revelation.

12. For more on the role of color in establishing and policing cultural hierarchies, see David Batchelor's Chromophobia (London: Reaktion Books, 2000).

13. "In Conversation: Donna Haraway with Thyrza Nichols Goodeve," *The Brooklyn Rail* (December 2017-January 2018). https://brooklynrail.org/2017/12/artDONNA-HARAWAY-with-Thyrza-Nichols-Goodeve

14. Wall writes in the same essay, "Photography and Liquid Intelligence," "By calling water an 'archaism' here I mean that it embodies a memory trace of very ancient production processes—of washing, bleaching, dissolving and so on, which are connected to the origin of techè—like the separation of ores in primitive mining, for example."

15. Elizabeth Grosz, *Becoming Undone: Darwinian Reflections on Life, Politics, and Art*, (Durham, NC: Duke University Press, 2011), p. 172.

16. For more, read *Lynn Margulis, Symbiotic Planet: A New Look at Evolution* (New York: Basic Books, 2008).

17. Grosz, ibid, p. 173, 182.

18. Ibid. p. 176

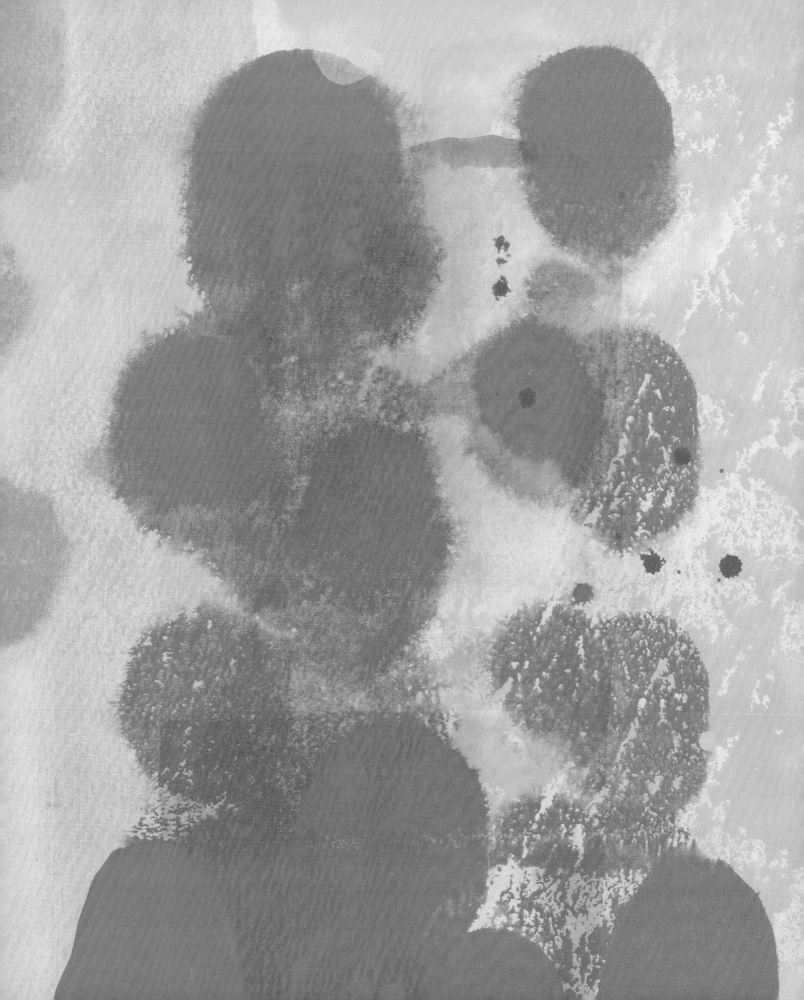

Long Impulse (#03-22), 2022
Acrylic on linen
72 x 66 inches
182.9 x 167.6 cm

Long Impulse (#04-22), 2022
Acrylic on linen
72 x 66 inches
182.9 x 167.6 cm

Round and Round (#05-22), 2022
Acrylic on linen
72 x 66 inches
182.9 x 167.6 cm

Blue Moon (#06-22), 2022
Acrylic on linen
72 x 66 inches
182.9 x 167.6 cm

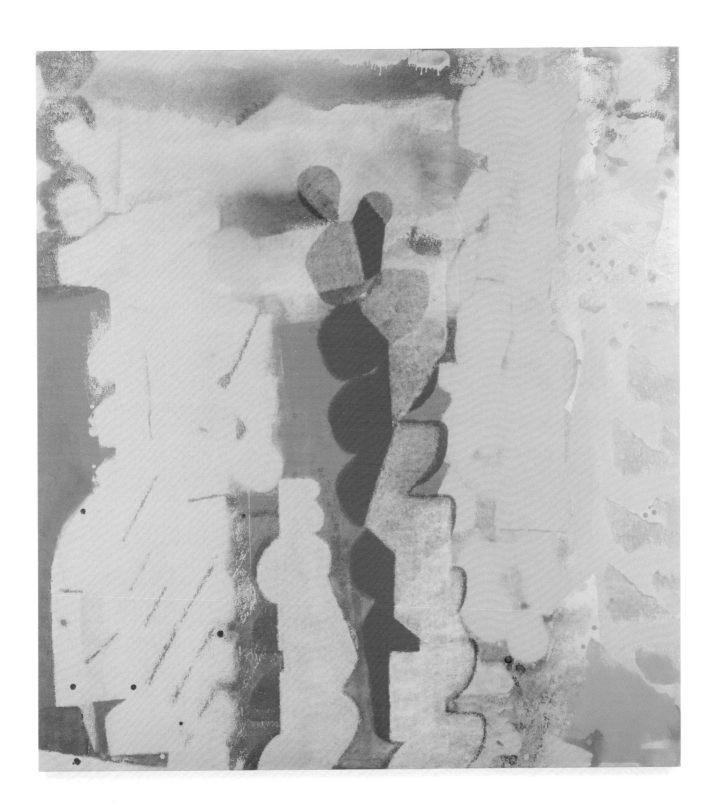

Untitled (#07-22), 2022
Acrylic on mural cloth
52 x 52 inches
132.1 x 132.1 cm

Serpentine Swell (#08-22), 2022
Acrylic on mural cloth
74 x 68 inches
188 x 172.7 cm

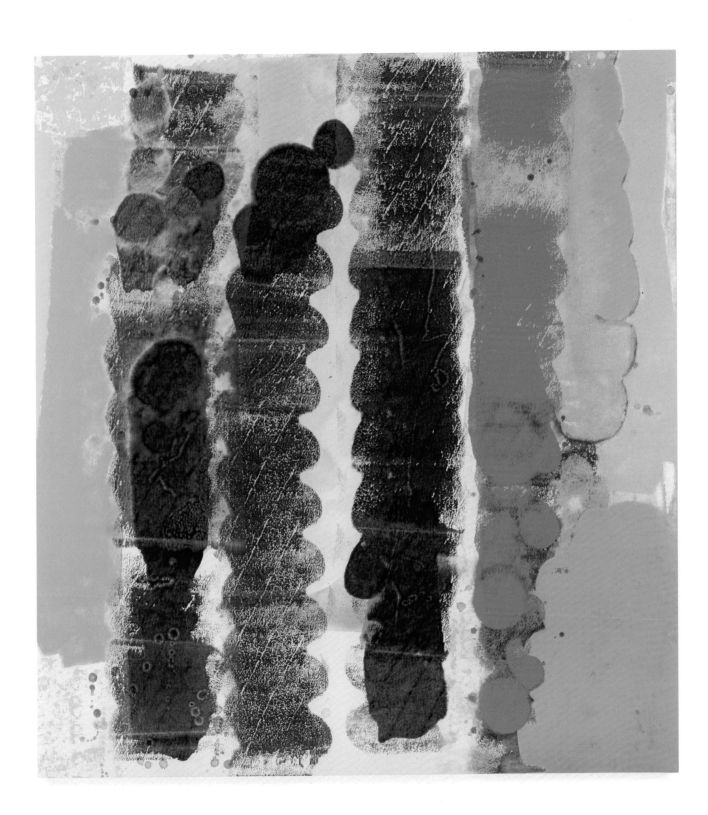

Twist Turns (#09-22), 2022
Acrylic on mural cloth
74 x 68 inches
188 x 172.7 cm

Wild Is The Wind (#10-22), 2022
Acrylic on mural cloth
72 x 60 inches
182.9 x 152.4 cm

Play It As It Lays (#11-22), 2022
Acrylic on linen
76 x 84 inches
193 x 213.4 cm

Untitled (#12-22), 2022
Acrylic on linen
72 x 66 inches
182.9 x 167.6 cm

Untitled (#13-22), 2022
Acrylic on mural cloth
72 x 66 inches
182.9x 167.6 cm

Near Swarm (#14-22), 2023
Acrylic on linen
40 x 40 inches
101.6 x 101.6 cm

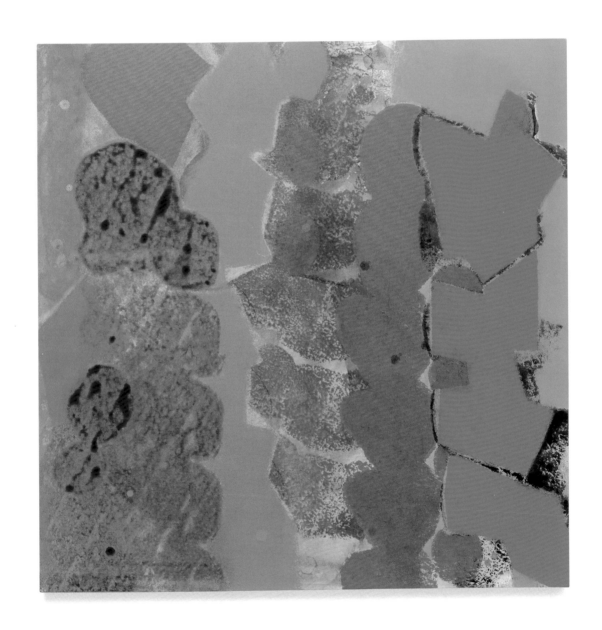

Near Swarm (#15-22), 2023
Acrylic on linen
40 x 40 inches
101.6 x 101.6 cm

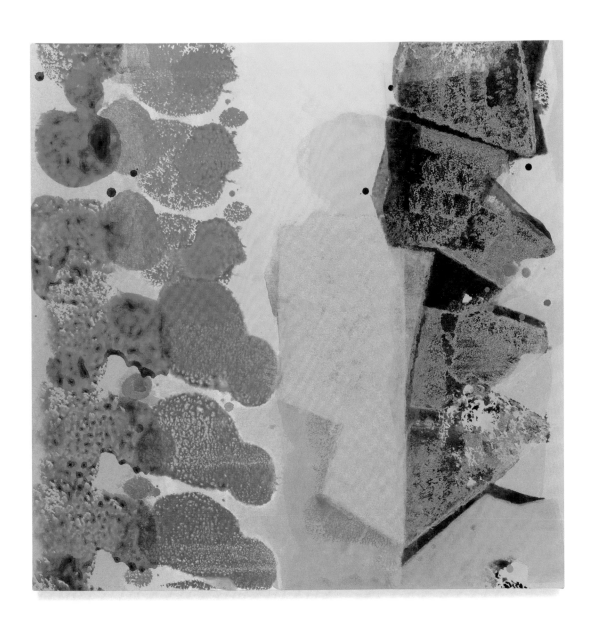

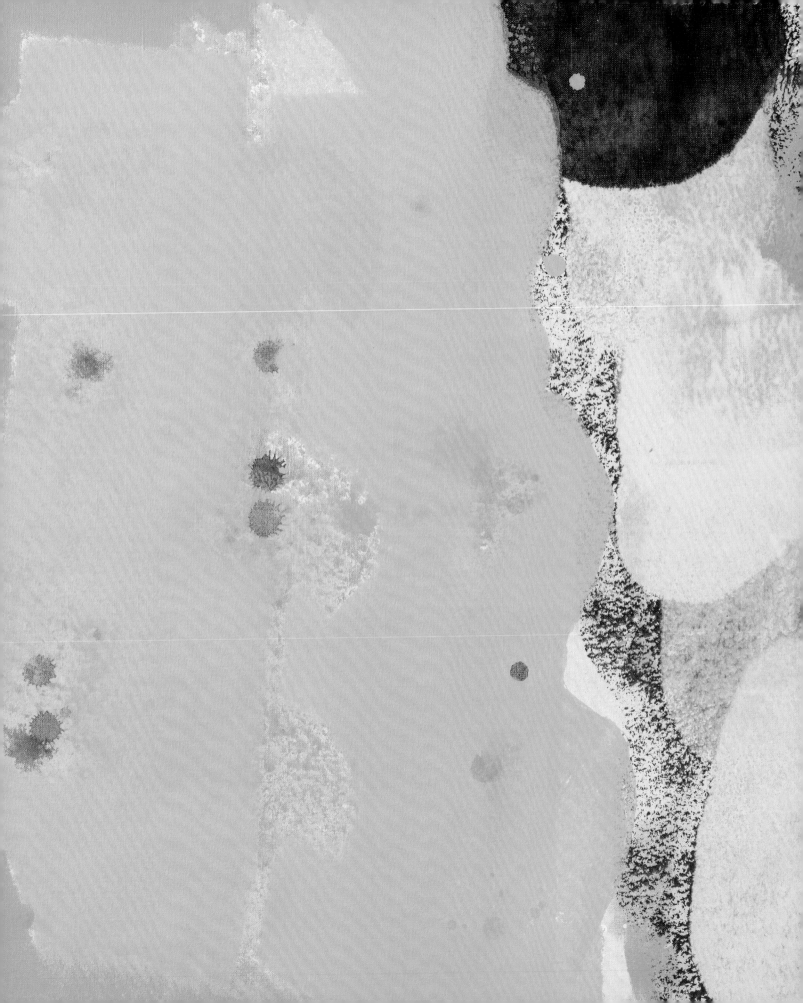

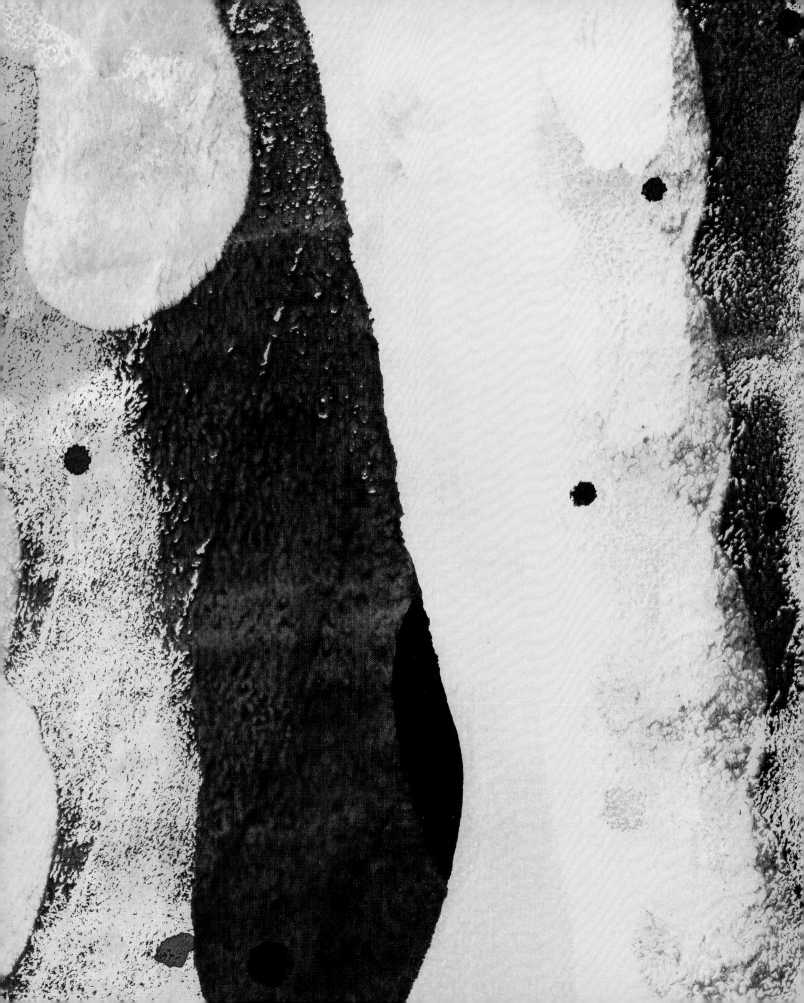

YUNHEE MIN

Born in Seoul, Korea in 1962
Lives and works in Los Angeles, CA

EDUCATION

2008
MDes, Graduate School of Design, Harvard University,
    Cambridge, MA

1994
Kunstakademie, Düsseldorf, Germany

1991
BFA, ArtCenter College of Design, Pasadena, CA

SOLO EXHIBITIONS

2023
"New Paintings," Miles McEnery Gallery, New York, NY

2021
"Vitreous Opacities," Vielmetter Los Angeles, Los Angeles, CA

2020
"Peggy Ahwesh: Heart_Land," JOAN Gallery, Los Angeles, CA
"Up Close in Distance" (online exhibition), Gallery Platform
    LA, Los Angeles, CA
"For Instance," Re-siting modification, Wallis Annenberg
    Terrace, Hammer Museum, Los Angeles, CA

2019
"Up Close in Distance (bars, flags, pools)," Hammer Museum,
    Los Angeles, CA

2018
"Wilde Paintings," Susanne Vielmetter Los Angeles Projects,
    Los Angeles, CA

2016
"Movements," Ameringer | McEnery | Yohe, New York, NY

2015
"Luminaire Delirium (Equitablelife or soft machine),"
    Equitable Vitrines, Los Angeles, CA
"movements," Susanne Vielmetter Los Angeles Projects,
    Culver City, CA

2013
"Into the Sun," Susanne Vielmetter Los Angeles Projects,
    Culver City, CA
"Shades for Night," installation, Night Gallery, Los Angeles, CA

2012
"Spectra: fixtures, attachments, and ornamentals," Exercise,
    Vancouver, Canada
"For Instance," Lindbrook Terrace, Hammer Museum,
    Los Angeles, CA

2010
"Attraction," Susanne Vielmetter Los Angeles Projects,
    Culver City, CA

2009
"Continuum: Structure #003," LAXART, Los Angeles, CA

2008
"Recent Paintings," James Harris Gallery, Seattle, WA
"For instance," Amie and Tony James Gallery, The City
    University of New York, New York, NY

2006
"Above and Beyond," Pasadena Museum of Contemporary
    Art, Pasadena, CA

2005
"Distance is like the future," Circa Series, Museum of
    Contemporary Art San Diego, San Diego, CA
"Another Country," Susanne Vielmetter Los Angeles
    Projects, Culver City, CA

2004
"Difference and Repetition (Invisible Cities)," Microsoft
    Corporation at Redmond, Redmond, WA
"Fading Wild," Finesilver Gallery, San Antonio, TX
"Double Positive," Artpace, San Antonio, TX

2003
James Harris Gallery, Seattle, WA
"out of bounds (from near and afar)," Yerba Buena Center
    for the Arts, San Francisco, CA
"Corrugate," Susanne Vielmetter Los Angeles Projects,
    Los Angeles, CA

2002
"Events in Dense Fog," Luckman Gallery, California State
    University, Los Angeles, CA

2001
"Recline," James Harris Gallery, Seattle, WA

2000
ACME., Los Angeles, CA

1999
"I put a spell on you too," Plug In, Winnipeg, Canada
"Tugboat," Sala Diaz, San Antonio, TX

1998
"Work in two and three dimensions," Post, Los Angeles, CA
"Windows on Wilshire" (curated by Howard Fox),
    Los Angeles County Museum of Art, Los Angeles, CA

1997
"One foot in front of the other," Or Gallery, Vancouver, Canada
"Home Improvement Paintings," Lasca, Los Angeles, CA
"Between the Sheets," The Full Moon Gallery, Foundation
    for Art Resources, Los Angeles, CA
"Agent Orange," Post, Los Angeles, CA

1996
"Fast times," ACME., Santa Monica, CA

1995
Domestic Setting, Culver City, CA

GROUP EXHIBITIONS

2021
"20 Years," Vielmetter Los Angeles, Los Angeles, CA

2019
"The Light Touch," Vielmetter Los Angeles, Los Angeles, CA
"Art in Embassies Exhibition," US Embassy Copenhagen,
    Copenhagen, Denmark

2018
"Belief in Giants," Miles McEnery Gallery, New York, NY
"Yunhee Min & Peter Tolkin: Red Carpet in C," University of
    California, Riverside, Riverside, CA

2015
"Elemental | Seeing the Light," Stuart Haaga Gallery,
    Descanso Gardens, Los Angeles, CA
"Magic Mountain," Museum of Contemporary Art Santa
    Barbara Satellite, Santa Barbara, CA
"Speed Space" (curated by Alexandra Gaty), Tif Sigfrids,
    Los Angeles, CA

2013
"Spectra," San Diego State University Downtown Gallery,
    San Diego, CA
"Nacker Gläubigen" (curated by Davida Nemeroff),
    Infernoesque//Pascal Richter, Berlin, Germany
"The Object Salon" (curated by Calvin Marcus), Roberts
    & Tilton Gallery, Culver City, CA

2012
"Lost Line," Los Angeles County Museum of Art,
    Los Angeles, CA
"Vis-à-vis Visitation Field" (curated by Aaron Wrinkle),
    Cirrus Gallery, Los Angeles, CA

2011
"WP9: Yunhee Min, Patrick Meagher, Miles Coolidge," Night
    Gallery, Los Angeles, CA
"Plain Brown Wrapper" (curated by Statler Waldorf Gallery),
    Human Resources, Los Angeles, CA
"Night Gallery at The Chateau Marmont," Bar Marmont,
    Los Angeles, CA
"Painting in Parts" (curated by Michael Klein), Maryland Art
    Place, Baltimore, MD

2009
"ABCyz," Silvershed Gallery, New York, NY

2008
"Claire Cowie: 12 Views || Yunhee Min: New Paintings,"
James Harris Gallery, Seattle, WA
"People Weekly," The Amie and Tony James Gallery,
The City University of New York, New York, NY
"Digital With Monument," Silvershed Gallery, New York, NY

2007
"Merit Badge 2" (curated by Jason Middlebrook), Rockland
Center for the Arts, West Nyack, NY
"The Trans-Aestheticization of Daily Life" (curated by Peter
Zeller), Sweeney Art Gallery, Riverside, CA
"Swell Ground," Rockland Center for the Arts, West Nyack, NY

2006
"Too Much Love" (curated by Amy Adler), Angles Gallery,
Los Angeles, CA

2005
"Around About Abstraction," Weatherspoon Art Museum,
Greensboro, NC
"Wall Painting" (curated by Frances Colpitt), University of
Texas, San Antonio, TX
Korean American Museum, Los Angeles, CA

2004
"Difference and Repetition (Invisible Cities)," Microsoft
Corporation at Redmond, Remond, WA
"New," Susanne Vielmetter Los Angeles Projects, Culver
City, CA
"Yunhee Min – Herbert Hamak," ArtSource, San Francisco, CA

2003
"Warped Space" (curated by Ralph Rugoff), Wattis Institute
for Contemporary Arts, San Francisco, CA
"International Abstraction: Making Painting Real" (curated by
Lisa Corrin), Seattle Art Museum, Seattle, WA
"Abstraction" (curated by Eungie Joo), Artist Space,
New York, NY
"Cal's Art," University of North Texas Art Gallery, Denton, TX

2001
"Fresh: Altoids Curiously Strong Collection," New Museum,
New York, NY
"Rogue Wave," L.A. Louver Gallery, Venice, CA
"Snap Shot," Hammer Museum, Los Angeles, CA; traveled to
Museum of Contemporary Art, North Miami, FL

2000
"The Next Wave" (curated by Noriko Gamblin), California
Center for the Arts, Escondido, Escondido, CA
"KOREAMERICAKOREA," Sonje Museum of Contemporary
Art, Seoul, Korea; traveled to KyungJu, Korea
"Deterritorialization of Process" (curated by Michael Joo),
Artists Space, New York, NY
"Shimmer" (curated by Thomas Lawson), Municipal Art
Gallery, Barnsdall Art Park, Los Angeles, CA

1999
"Hubcap Diamond Star Halo," Claremont Graduate
University, Peggy Phelps Gallery, Claremont, CA
"Other Paintings" (curated by Julie Joyce), Huntington
Beach Art Center, Los Angeles, CA
"Structural Elements, Views of Architectural Elements,"
Transamerica Pyramid, San Francisco, CA
"Under 500/Intimate Abstract Painting" (curated by James
Hayward), Black Dragon Society, Los Angeles, CA
"After the Goldrush" (curated by Joe Wallin & Lea
Gongitano), Thread Waxing Space, New York, NY

1998
"Wings of Desire" (curated by Michelle Guy), San Francisco
Art Institute, San Francisco, CA
"Windows on Wilshire" (curated by Howard Fox), Los
Angeles County Museum of Art, Los Angeles, CA

1997
"Yunhee Min/Lise Soskolne," Or Gallery, Vancouver, Canada
W139, Amsterdam, Netherlands
"Agent Orange (Elevator Installation)," POST, Los Angeles, CA
"Ambient Suburbs" (curated by Julie Joyce), POST,
Los Angeles

1996

"Human Condition" (curated by Bennett Roberts), Caren
Golden Fine Art, New York, NY

The Full Moon Gallery at the Foundation for Art Resources
(FAR), Los Angeles, CA

1994

"Current Abstractions," Los Angeles Municipal Art Gallery,
Barnsdall Art Park, Los Angeles, CA

"Rundgang," Kunstakademie Düsseldorf, Düsseldorf,
Germany

AWARDS

2022

Fellowship, John Simon Guggenheim Memorial Foundation,
New York, NY

2016

Grant Recipient, Creative Capacity Fund Quick Grant
Program, Los Angeles, CA

Finalist (with Peter Tolkin Architecture), Glenarm
Powerplant Public Art Project, Pasadena, CA

2015

University of California Institute for Research in the Arts for
a Major Grant, Riverside, CA

2013

Storefront for Art and Architecture Residency, Silvershed
invited by Peter Zellner, New York, NY

2010

Aurobora Press, San Francisco, CA

2009

Artist in Residence, Jeju Museum of Contemporary Art,
Jeju-Do, South Korea

2008

Certificate of Distinction in Teaching, Derek Bok Center,
Harvard University, Cambridge, MA

2006

Alpert Ucross Residency Prize, Clearmont, WY

2003

Wattis Artist in Residence, Yerba Buena Center for the Arts,
San Francisco, CA

1999

City of Los Angeles Cultural Affairs Individual Artist Grant,
Los Angeles, CA

1996

Individual Artist Grant, Korea Arts Foundation of America,
Los Angeles, CA

SELECT COLLECTIONS

Altoids Collection, New Museum, New York, NY

Hammer Museum, Los Angeles, CA

Los Angeles County Museum of Art, Los Angeles, CA

Museum of Contemporary Art San Diego, La Jolla, CA

Nerman Museum of Contemporary Art, Overland Park, KS

Seattle Art Museum, Seattle, WA

Stuart Collection, University of California San Diego,
La Jolla, CA

University of Puget Sound, Tacoma, WA

Published on the occasion of the exhibition

YUNHEE MIN

16 March – 22 April 2023

Miles McEnery Gallery
520 West 21st Street
New York NY 10011

tel +1 212 445 0051
www.milesmcenery.com

Publication © 2023 Miles McEnery Gallery
All rights reserved
Essay © 2022 Nick Herman

Director of Exhibitions
Anastasija Jevtovic, New York, NY

Publications and Archival Assistant
Julia Schlank, New York, NY

Photography by
Christopher Burke Studio, Los Angeles, CA

Color separations by
Echelon, Los Angeles, CA

Catalogue layout by
McCall Associates, New York, NY

ISBN: 978-0-9850184-1-2

Cover: *Blue Moon (#06-22), (detail)*, 2022

MILES
McENERY
GALLERY